INTERFACT

THE BOOK AND DISK **THAT WORK TOGETHER**

RAINFORESTS

Created by
Two-Can Publishing Ltd
346 Old Street
London
EC1V 9NQ

Disk
Creative Director: Jason Page
Programming Director: Brett Cropley
Art Director: Sarah Evans
Senior Designer: James Evans
Programmer: Paul Steven
Sub Editor: Jo Keane
Consultant: Terry Hudson
Illustrators: Rhiannon Cackett, Jeffrey Lewis,
Carlo Tartaglia, Nick Ward, Simon Woolford
Production Manager: Joya Bart-Plange

Book
Creative Director: Jason Page
Editors: Kate Graham, Jo Keane, Alison Woodhouse
Author: Lucy Baker
Consultant: Terry Hudson
Art Director: Belinda Webster
Designers: Michele Egar, David Oh
Production Manager: Joya Bart-Plange

This edition published in 1997 in association with
Franklin Watts
96 Leonard Street
London
EC2A 4RH

MAC ISBN 1-85434-475-7
PC ISBN 1-85434-463-3
CD ISBN 1-85434-487-0

Dewey Decimal Classification 574.5

2 4 6 8 10 9 7 5 3 1

A catalogue record for this book is available from the British Library

Printed in Hong Kong by Wing King Tong

Photograph Credits: front cover Planet Earth Pictures
p.9 Bruce Coleman p.11 (top) Heather Angel/Biofotos (bottom) South American Pictures/Tony Morrison p.12 Bruce
Coleman/E. & P. Bauer p.13 Ardea/Pat Morris p.14 (top) Ardea/Anthony & Elizabeth Bomford (bottom) Bruce Coleman/
J. Mackinnon p.15 (top) NHPA/L.H. Newman (centre) Bruce Coleman (right) NHPA/Jany Sauvanet Library/
J. Von Puttkamer p.16 (bottom) Ardea (top) Bruce Coleman p.17 Bruce Coleman p.18 The Hutchinson Library/J. Von
Puttkamer p.19 (top) Survival International Steve Cox (bottom) The Hutchinson Library/J. Von Puttkamer p.20 Bruce
Coleman/Michael Fogden p.21 Survival International Victor Englebert p.22 Impact Photos p.23 The Hutchinson Library
pp.24–25 NHPA p.26 Oxford Scientific Films/R.A. Acharya p.27 South American Pictures/Bill Leimbach
p.35 Impact/Julie Eckhardt. Illustrations by Francis Mosley. Story illustrated by Valerie McBride.

INTERFACT™

THE BOOK AND DISK THAT WORK TOGETHER

INTERFACT will have you hooked in minutes – and that's a fact!

● The disk is packed with interactive activities, puzzles, quizzes and games that are fun to do and packed with interesting facts.

Try building an interactive food web and discover what different creatures eat.

Dead plants and animals

● Open the book and discover more fascinating information highlighted with lots of full-colour illustrations and photographs.

Gifts from the forest

Rainforest tribes can get everything they need from their homeland. The many different plants and animals found in the forest provide raw materials for meals, houses, clothes, medicines, tools and cosmetics.

We also use rainforest products. Many of the fruits, nuts and cereals that fill our supermarket shelves originated in the rainforest. The domestic chicken, which is now farmed worldwide, began life on the forest floor. The most expensive **hardwoods**, such as teak, mahogany and ebony, come from rainforest trees.

Other rainforest products include tea, coffee, cocoa, rubber and many types of medicine.

We know very little about the rainforests. Scientists believe there are thousands of future foodstuffs, medicines and other raw materials waiting to be discovered.

▼ These frogs produce a strong poison under their skin to stop other animals from eating them. Some tribes extract this poison by roasting the frogs and collecting their sweat. They use it to tip their blow-pipe darts when they hunt.

● A quarter of all medicines owe their origins to rainforest plants and animals.

● Rainforest insects could offer an alternative to expensive pesticides. In Florida, three kinds of wasp were successfully introduced to control pests that were damaging the citrus trees.

● There are at least 1,500 potential new fruits and vegetables growing in the world's rainforests.

▲ Yanomami tribesmen hunt game, while women search the forest floor for food.

Read up and find out about all the products of the rainforest.

● To get the most out of **INTERFACT** use the book and disk together. Look out for the special signs, called Disk Links and Bookmarks. To find out more, turn to page 43.

23

BOOKMARK

DISK LINK
How can we use rainforest plants? Find out when you play Flora Flip.

Once you've clicked on to **INTERFACT** you'll never look back.

LOAD UP!
Go to **page 40** to find out how to load your disks and click into action.

What's on the disk

HELP SCREEN

Learn how to use the disk in no time at all.

These are the controls the Help Screen will tell you how to use:
- arrow keys
- reading boxes
- "hot" words

ROAM AROUND THE RAINFOREST

Explore the exciting world of the rainforest.

Throw yourself into the deepest, darkest depths of the rainforest with this interactive screen. Be careful where you click your mouse – who knows what might be lurking there!

FOOD FOR THOUGHT

What is a food web and how does it keep the rainforest alive?

Learn about the eating habits of rainforest animals by building a forest food web. Discover which creatures are prey and which are predators.

WORD UP

Save the monkey by guessing the mystery rainforest word.

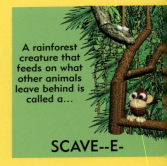

Think fast to save the monkey from the jaws of the hungry snake! Work out the mystery rainforest words before the monkey becomes a tasty snack!

CREATE A RAINFOREST

Design and build the rainforest of your dreams!

Design your own lush rainforest, full of plants and creatures! Select which items you want to use, position them, then print out your picture to colour in and keep.

IT'S A JUNGLE OUT THERE

What does the future hold for the world's rainforests?

Meet Tommy the tamarin and Squawk the scarlet macaw! Tommy has the answers to all Squawk's questions about the rainforests. Just click your mouse to find out more.

FLORA FLIP

Name the plants and learn about their uses.

Play this interactive card game and match the plants with their names. Once you've got them all right, you'll discover how useful they really are.

GO BANANAS!

Are you an all-round rainforest expert?

Put your knowledge of the rainforest to the test and see how many bananas you can earn. Then enter a banana-throwing competition!

What's in the book

Looking at rainforests

Imagine a forest unchanged for 60 million years, where giant trees reach up to the sky, their leafy branches blocking out light to the forest floor below. Imagine a place where the temperature hardly changes from day to night, season to season, year to year. A place where rain clouds hang in the air and heavy downpours are common. The rainforest is that amazing place.

Inside the rainforest, as much as two-thirds of all land-based animals and plants can be found. People have lived deep in the heart of rainforests for thousands of years too.

DISK LINK

Have a wild time planting your own lush tropical rainforest in Create A Rainforest.

DID YOU KNOW?

● Rainforests are the wettest areas of land in the world. As much as 6m of rain may fall during a single year in some places.

● Almost half of all rainforests have been cut down in the last 50 years and the clearance goes on. Scientists estimate that around 20 million hectares are destroyed every year.

LAYERS OF THE RAINFOREST

Most rainforest life is found about 40m above the ground, in a layer called the **canopy**. This is where the branches of the giant trees tangle together to form a lush, green platform.

Underneath the canopy, little grows in the darkness. Where light does break through, smaller plants compete for space. Leaves that rain down from the canopy are converted into food by insects and animals.

canopy

understorey

forest floor

Where in the world

Over half of the world's rainforests are in South and Central America. The remainder can be found in parts of Africa, Asia and Australia. Almost all rainforests lie between two imaginary lines north and south of the **equator**, called the **Tropic of Cancer** and the **Tropic of Capricorn**. This is why they are often called tropical rainforests.

It has been hot and wet in the tropics for millions of years. These constant conditions have made it possible for rainforests to develop into the most diverse and complex **environments** in the world. Some scientists recognise over 40 different types of rainforest, each with its own variety of plant and animal life.

Rainforests once formed a wide, green belt around the planet, but today, pictures taken from space tell a different story. All around the world large areas of rainforest are vanishing as people clear the way for crops, homes and businesses. Many species of wildlife are disappearing too.

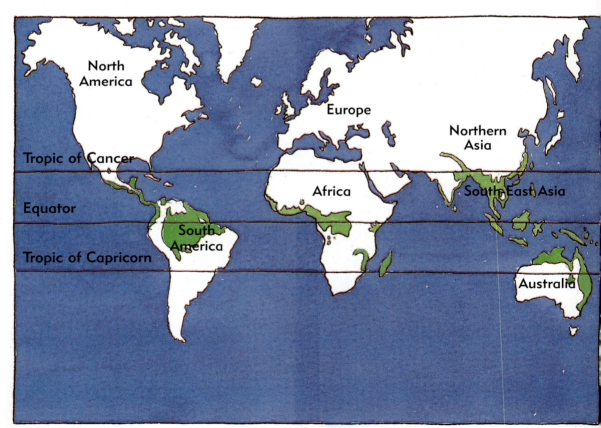

North America

Europe

Northern Asia

Tropic of Cancer

Africa

South East Asia

Equator

South America

Tropic of Capricorn

Australia

▶ In the tropics, the only change in weather conditions is from wet to wetter during the rainy season. This means that rainforest trees do not need to flower in spring or shed their leaves in autumn. Each type of tree has its own growth cycle which guarantees a regular supply of fruits, nuts and seeds for all the creatures.

▼ The largest rainforest in the world stretches across the Amazon Basin in South America. It covers an area nearly as big as Australia. The Amazon River, which snakes through this rainforest, is the largest river system in the world.

The plant bank

In the rainforest, there can be over 179 species of tree in a single acre of land.

Rainforests contain a huge variety of other plants too. Wherever light reaches the forest floor, an exotic layer of herbs and ferns flourish. Wiry stems hang around the giant tree trunks. These climbers and vines produce a mass of leaves and flowers in the canopy layer.

The canopy is like a huge aerial garden. Many types of moss, lichen and flowering plants covering the branches are called **epiphytes**. Their roots dangle freely or grow in a thin layer of compost which forms in the cracks of branches.

▲ The rafflesia grows on the forest floor in parts of Asia. It produces flowers up to 1m across – the biggest in the world. They have thick, warty petals and spiky centres that stink of rotting meat.

▶ Water collects in some epiphytes and provides ponds for tiny rainforest frogs.

DISK LINK
Find out more about the rainforest's exotic plants and put your memory to the test by playing Flora Flip.

PLANT FACTS

● Rainforest trees have shallow root systems. To prevent them falling over, the trees often grow special **buttress roots**.

● Most rainforest leaves are thick and waxy with special **drip-tips** to drain away water. They are often so big they can be used as umbrellas.

Feasting in the forest

The lush vegetation of the rainforests is home to millions of different insects and creepy crawlies. Some, such as flies and beetles, act as cleaners, clearing the forest floor of debris. Others, such as wasps and bees, help to pollinate the flowers of the forest. There are lots of ants and spiders too. Between them, they eat many other insects and so stop them becoming too plentiful.

The plants and insects of the rainforest provide thousands of different animals with food to eat. Here are some of them.

▲ Lizards live all over the rainforest, eating insects, plants and occasionally, small animals. Most lizards seize insects in their mouths, but a few snatch them from the air with their extra-long tongues.

◀ Orang-utans, found in the rainforests of Borneo and Sumatra in South-East Asia, have huge appetites. They love fruit, but also chew leaves, shoots, tree bark and, occasionally, take eggs from birds' nests. Orang-utans' long, powerful arms and hook-shaped hands make swinging through the tree tops easy work.

DISK LINK
Read these pages carefully. Then show off your brain power in Go Bananas!

▲ Bats are common in the rainforests. They are the world's only flying mammals. Many bats hunt insects but some, such as the flying fox above, eat fruit. Fruit bats help to spread seeds around the forest.

▲ The hummingbird's long, thin bill is ideal for reaching the sweet nectar found inside flowers, but these birds also eat insects. Hummingbirds are flying experts and can even fly backwards!

▶ Sloths have strict leaf-eating diets. They spend practically all their time in the tree tops. There are two-toed sloths and three-toed sloths, such as the one here. Algae and insects live in the sloth's fur.

Forest fiends

The rainforest is a dangerous place. The brightly-coloured parrots, chattering monkeys and slumbering sloths may seem carefree but they have their enemies. When a giant eagle soars overhead or an agile cat is on the prowl, the whole canopy is gripped in terror.

Big cats and eagles are the largest hunters in the forest, but there are hundreds of others. In the canopy, long, slender tree snakes catch lizards, frogs and small birds. On the forest floor, huge, heavy constrictors, such as the anaconda, wait for larger prey, such as wild boar or deer that forage around in the leaf litter.

Some of the most deadly creatures are the smaller ones. Scorpions, spiders, bees and wasps are found all over the forest. Many have poisonous bites or stings that can cause rashes, sickness, or, in extreme circumstances, death.

▲ Each rainforest has its own type of giant eagle. In Africa it is the crowned eagle, in South America, the harpy eagle and in Asia, the monkey-eating eagle, shown here. Giant eagles catch monkeys and sloths in the canopy layer.

◄ Some forest cats, such as margays, chase squirrels through the **understorey**. Others, such as this jaguar, wait on low branches and pounce on passing animals underneath.

◀ The feared bushmaster hunts small animals that **scavenge** on the South American forest floor.

DISK LINK
Food For Thought will tell you which animal is at the top of the food web.

PROTECTION FROM PERIL

● The smallest rainforest creatures have the greatest number of natural enemies, so it is not surprising that they have developed many ways to defend themselves, including **camouflage**.

● Some creatures produce a poison which makes them unpleasant to eat. Bold markings advertise the fact and predators learn to recognise the warning signs.

● Some butterflies have hidden eyespots on their wings. They flash these false eyes at attackers, startling them, so that the butterflies may be able to escape.

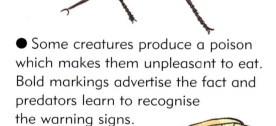

● Bush crickets use clever camouflage to reduce the risk of being eaten.

Rainforest people

Outsiders are uncomfortable in the rainforest. They find the hot, humid conditions stifling. Every step they take is fraught with danger and although there is food all around them, they cannot tell a poisonous berry from a nutritious and refreshing fruit.

Certain groups of people have lived in the rainforests for thousands of years. To them, the rainforest is home and the only world they know. Rainforest **tribes** live in structured communities with their own cultures and customs. They have a very deep understanding of the way the rainforests work. They know which plants and animals are useful and how to take from the forest without harming it.

There are rainforest tribes in parts of Africa, Asia and South America, but their way of life is threatened. Although they have rights according to international laws, they are often mistreated and their land is stolen or invaded. If all the ancient tribes disappear, their knowledge of the rainforest may be lost forever.

▼ A large area of rainforest can support only a few hundred people, so tribes are spread thinly. Some build communal houses, where many families live together.

◀ Rainforest children do not have to go to school, but they still have a lot to learn. Their elders must teach them everything there is to know about life in the rainforest.

▼ Many rainforest people paint their bodies with colourful dyes and use feathers, flowers and other natural materials to make simple pieces of jewellery.

PEOPLE FACTS

● The Pygmy people of the African rainforest are very small. The tallest of them are only some 1.4m tall.

● Life is not easy in the rainforest. A person in the modern world may live for over 70 years. In the rainforest, few people survive more than 40 years. Diseases, such as flu and measles, introduced by European settlers, are still big killers of native tribes. Over 80 different tribes have died out in Brazil since 1900.

DISK LINK
Word Up quizzes you on all the new words in this book — and at least one of them is on this page!

Gifts from the forest

Rainforest tribes can get everything they need from their homeland. The many different plants and animals found in the forest provide raw materials for meals, houses, clothes, medicines, tools and cosmetics.

We also use rainforest products. Many of the fruits, nuts and cereals that fill our supermarket shelves originated in the rainforest. The domestic chicken, which is now farmed worldwide, began life on the forest floor. The most expensive **hardwoods**, such as teak, mahogany and ebony, come from rainforest trees.

Other rainforest products include tea, coffee, cocoa, rubber and many types of medicine.

We still know very little about the rainforests. Scientists believe there are thousands of future foodstuffs, medicines and other raw materials waiting to be discovered.

▼ These frogs produce a strong poison under their skin to stop other animals from eating them. Some tribes extract this poison by roasting the frogs and collecting their sweat. They use it to tip their blow-pipe darts when they hunt.

RAINFOREST TREASURES

● There is an Amazonian tree that produces a sap very similar to diesel. It can be poured straight into a truck's tank and used as fuel.

● A quarter of all medicines owe their origins to rainforest plants and animals.

● Rainforest insects could offer an alternative to expensive pesticides. In Florida, three kinds of wasp were successfully introduced to control pests that were damaging the citrus trees.

● There are at least 1,500 potential new fruits and vegetables growing in the world's rainforests.

▲ Yanomami tribesmen hunt game, while women search the forest floor for food.

Rainforest destruction

Rainforests are natural treasure houses but they are being destroyed for nothing more than timber and the land on which they stand. This is because most rainforests are found in poor, developing countries. These countries cannot afford to keep their beautiful forests.

Large areas of rainforest are sold to timber companies. They send bulldozers and chainsaw gangs into the forest to cut down the hardwood trees. The wildlife flees and, although only the oldest and largest trees are felled, over half of the forest may be damaged by the time all the work is finished.

Rainforests are cleared completely to reach rich mineral reserves, such as iron, copper or uranium, or to make huge cash-crop plantations of coffee, cocoa or bananas.

Big business is only half the story. There are thousands of poor, homeless people in rainforest countries who are encouraged to leave the overcrowded cities and go and farm pieces of rainforest land. They are called **slash-and-burn** farmers because they build simple homesteads in the forest and then burn the surrounding vegetation to enrich the soil.

DISK LINK
Learn more about rainforest destruction when you play It's A Jungle Out There.

▼ Around 500 million people have moved into the rainforests. These newcomers clear the forest to farm small areas of land.

DID YOU KNOW?

● Industrial countries buy over 18 times more hardwood today than they did 50 years ago.

● Over half of Central America's rainforests have gone. They have been cleared to build huge cattle ranches. Much of the meat produced is sold to western countries to feed the demands of their growing burger markets.

▶ See the difference between the distant lush, green rainforest and the lifeless, cracked earth in the foreground. Huge areas of Brazil have been devastated and animals and plants are gone forever.

Paradise lost

It can take less than 10 years for rainforest land to become as barren and lifeless as a desert. This is because most rainforests grow in poor clay soils. Only a thin layer of nutritious **topsoil** covers the forest floor and this is anchored down by giant tree trunks.

When slash-and-burn farmers clear rainforest land to grow their crops, they destroy the trees that are needed to keep the soil in place. After only a few years, the tropical rains wash the topsoil away and the land becomes too difficult to cultivate.

FROM GOOD TO BAD

● Trees and plants help to clean the air. They use sunlight, water and air to make food. In this process, they use the air that we breathe out (carbon dioxide) and produce the oxygen that we breathe in.

When rainforests are burnt to clear land, the fires create carbon dioxide which pollutes the air. The less trees there are, the less oxygen there is for us to live on.

The wastelands left by slash-and-burn farmers are baked dry by the sun and then drenched by the heavy rains. The rains, which would have watered the thirsty trees and plants, now fall straight to the ground and run downhill, carrying tons of soil with them. Valleys are flooded and rivers become clogged up with mud.

Scientists believe that, at the present rate of destruction, there will be no rainforests left by the year 2050. If this paradise is lost, several thousand different plants, trees and animals will disappear forever.

Save the rainforests

More and more people are becoming aware of the need to save the rainforests. Some steps have already been taken to slow down the rate of destruction. Native tribes have blocked the path of bulldozers and chainsaw gangs and many **conservation** groups have launched huge campaigns.

Much more could still be done. Timber companies could change the way they harvest the forest, to cut down the damage they cause. They could also replant areas of forest that have been disturbed. Slash-and-burn farmers could be taught to plant trees and crops together to preserve the fragile topsoil and use the same land for many years.

Rich, industrial countries could help too. They could reduce the debts owed to them by rainforest countries, which use their forest land to clear the debts. That way, at least the remaining forests could be preserved.

DISK LINK
Bet you can't guess what the orang-utan's name means. Roam Around The Rainforest and make it one of your discoveries!

▲ The Kayapo Indians live in the Amazon Rainforest in Brazil. Their traditional dress includes a piece of wood called a lip-plate which members of the tribe wear in holes cut in their lower lips. The Kayapo have campaigned hard to save the forest and their way of life from gold miners.

◀ Scientists believe that over 50 wild species of plants and animals become extinct every day because of rainforest destruction. Many of our favourite animals, such as tigers and orang-utans, are at risk because their homes are being destroyed. By protecting rainforests, they could be saved from **extinction**.

RAINFOREST ACTION

● Spread the word

Tell your friends and relatives about the plight of the rainforests. Write to the government asking it to help rainforest countries.

● Support rainforest campaigns

There are many charities and pressure groups trying to slow down the rate of rainforest destruction. They need money and support to continue their work. Watch out for news of how you can help them on television, radio or in newspapers and magazines.

The cowrie thieves

For thousands of years people have told stories
about the world around them. Often these stories try to
explain something that people do not really understand,
such as how the world began, or where light comes from.
This tale is told by the people of the Congo in Africa.

Long ago, in a village right in the middle
of the Congo, there lived a man and his
wife who were always causing mischief.

All the other villagers agreed that
these two had the most irritating habits.
They hardly ever did any work, preferring
to sit around and chatter to one another.
When they did start to work, they would
tire of whatever they were doing very
quickly and wander off to find something
else to do.

They were always dropping in at their
neighbours' huts, just when dinner was
ready. Their neighbours were obliged to
ask them in to supper, since that was
the local custom. But the worst thing
of all was the way they would pick up
other people's belongings.

The two of them would just wander into
other people's huts and start picking up
anything that they could see. They would
poke their noses into baskets, take a
mouthful of food or just move everything
around so that the owner of the hut
would come home to a terrible mess.

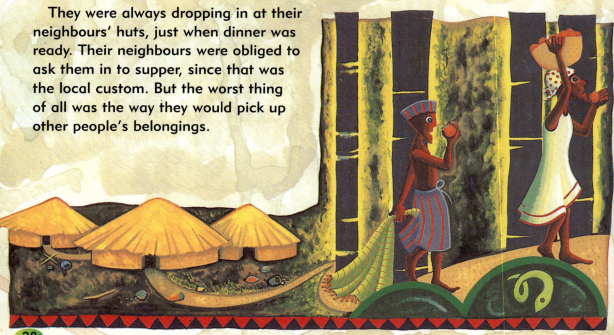

The other villagers put up with the pair because they never really did much harm. Whenever a villager lost his temper with them, they looked so hurt at the thought that they had done wrong and promised so fervently to mend their ways that it was impossible to be angry for long.

One day, however, they wandered into the hut of an important man in the village and pulled out his bag of cowrie shells, all his wealth, from under his bed. They tipped the cowrie shells out over the floor and began to play with them, counting them, rolling them around and making patterns on the floor.

Eventually the mischievous man decided to go and find some food, and his mischievous wife followed him, leaving the cowrie shells just as they were, all over the floor.

When the owner of the hut came back and saw his cowrie shells scattered about, his first thought was that he had been robbed.

He shouted to all the other villagers to come and see what had happened. The woman from the hut next door said that she had seen the mischievous man and his mischievous wife coming out of the important man's hut.

Just then, someone spotted the mischievous couple coming around the corner with a bunch of bananas. They looked very surprised when they were accused of stealing the cowrie shells.

The important man who thought he had been robbed did not wait for an explanation. "Just you wait until I get you!" he yelled.

He rushed at the pair, waving his arms fiercely. The mischievous man and his mischievous wife ran as fast as they could into the shelter of the forest, with all the villagers rushing after them.

When they reached the forest, the mischievous man and his mischievous wife climbed up a tree to hide from the villagers. For a few minutes the villagers chasing them were puzzled. Then one of them spotted the mischievous wife's hair hanging down from a branch.

"Let's sit up here and wait until they go away, and then go down," said the mischievous man.

But the villagers didn't go away. The important man who thought that he had been robbed, stood at the bottom of the tree and shouted: "Don't think you'll get away with it that easily!"

The villagers set a guard by the bottom of the tree, waiting for the mischievous man and his mischievous wife to give up and come down.

Time passed, and the villagers guarding the bottom of the tree changed twice a day, until all of them had guarded the tree once. The mischievous man and his mischievous wife sat in the tree, chattering to one another, and pulling fruit off the nearby branches. Their fingers and toes began to get very long and thin from gripping the branches and stretching out for fruit.

One day, when all the villagers had guarded the bottom of the tree twice, the mischievous man and his mischievous wife realised that the hair on their bodies had grown long and thick, making it hard for them to be seen in the branches.

Some time later, when all the villagers had guarded the bottom of the tree three times, the mischievous man and his mischievous wife felt a funny sensation at the bottom of their spines. They had grown tails! They jumped up and down on their branch, chattering to one another very fast, and swinging about with their new tails.

And that is why, even though the people of the Congo are often annoyed with mischievous monkeys who come into their houses and make a mess or take their food, they never harm them.

The villager at the bottom of the tree heard all the noise and stared up at the pair. What a surprise he got! The mischievous man and his mischievous wife had turned into monkeys!

When the villager went back to the village to tell the others what he had seen, the important man who thought he had been robbed was furious. But later, when he had counted his cowrie shells, he realised how unjust he had been. How he regretted his hastiness!

True or false?

Which of these facts are true and which are false?
If you have read this book carefully, you will know the answers!

1. Rainforests are found all over Europe.

2. Rainforests lie between the Tropics of Capricorn and Cancer.

3. There are up to 40 kinds of rainforest.

4. Orang-utans are found in the forests of Africa.

5. Over 179 tree species can grow in one acre of rainforest.

6. The world's largest rainforest is in Australia.

7. Algae and insects shelter in the long fur of the sloth.

8. Giant eagles feed on animals from the forest floor.

9. Chickens originally came from the rainforest.

10. Tribespeople collect poison from rainforest frogs by squeezing them.

11. Sap from an Amazonian tree can be used as diesel fuel in trucks.

12. The African Pygmies are some of the tallest people on Earth.

13. The rainforests may be destroyed by the year 2050.

ANSWERS: 1.F 2.T 3.T 4.F 5.T 6.F 7.T 8.F 9.T 10.F 11.T 12.F 13.T

Glossary

● **Buttress roots** develop to support the heavy trunks and help keep the tall trees of the rainforest upright.

● **Camouflage** is the method by which the surface of certain creatures is covered in patterns or colours matching their background. These help to hide them from predators. A chameleon can change its body colour according to the background it walks against.

● **Canopy** is the uppermost layer of the rainforest, the dense, leafy section some 6–7m deep, at 40–50m above ground. Most rainforest animals live in this layer.

● **Conservation** is the preservation of natural species and environments from exploitation by humans. This involves

● **Drip-tip** is the long tip on most leaves in the rainforest, developed to shed rain from the leaf's waxy surface.

● **Environment** is the particular combination of conditions in an area. This combination affects the type of living things, such as plants and animals, which inhabit it.

● **Epiphyte** is a plant growing on another plant without damaging it. It is not a parasite.

● **Equator** is the imaginary line lying exactly halfway between the North and South Poles. The majority of the world's rainforests are found directly north and south of this line.

● **Extinction** occurs when the last member of an animal or plant species dies out after overhunting, a change in its habitat or failure to compete with a new arrival in its niche.

● **Hardwood** trees such as ebony, teak and mahogany, grow in the rainforest. Their tough wood is excellent for making strong furniture and is in great demand. This is one cause of the destruction of large parts of the rainforest.

● **Scavenger** is a creature which feeds on the refuse left by others, for instance, on another animal's kill.

● **Tropic of Cancer, Tropic of Capricorn** are imaginary lines at about 23 degrees latitude north and south of the equator, at the point where the Sun changes its course over the Earth's surface. The area between these two lines is known as the Tropics and most rainforests are found in this region.

● **Understorey** is the name for the smaller trees and bushes which make up the middle level in a rainforest, below the tops of the taller trees.

● **Slash-and-burn** farming is practised by poor farmers who clear areas of the rainforest for soil on which to grow their crops. These farmers move on every few seasons as the soil holds little goodness once the trees have gone.

● **Topsoil** lies above the stony ground beneath the rainforest floor. This rich earth is held in place by the trees, but when they are cut down it is rapidly washed away by rains.

● **Tribe** is a community of people who live together for protection from danger and for a shared way of life.

Work book

Photocopy this sheet and use it to make your own notes.

Work book

Photocopy this sheet and use it to make your own notes.

Loading your INTERFACT disk

INTERFACT is available on floppy disk and CD-ROM for both PCs with Windows and Apple Macs. Make sure you follow the correct instructions for the disk you have chosen and your type of computer. Before you begin, check the minimum specification (inside front cover).

CD-ROM INSTRUCTIONS

If you have a copy of INTERFACT on CD, you can run the program from the disk – you don't need to install it on your hard drive.

PC WITH WINDOWS 95

1 Put the disk in the CD drive
2 Open MY COMPUTER
3 Double click on the CD drive icon
4 Double click on the icon called RAINFOR

PC WITH WINDOWS 3.1 OR 3.11

1 Put the disk in the CD drive
2 Select RUN from the FILE menu in the PROGRAM MANAGER
3 Type **D:\RAINFOR**
4 Press the RETURN key

APPLE MAC

1 Put the disk in the CD drive
2 Double click on the INTERFACT icon
3 Double click on the icon called RAINFOR

FLOPPY DISK INSTRUCTIONS

If you have a copy of INTERFACT on floppy disk you must install the program on to your computer's hard drive before you can run it.

PC WITH WINDOWS 3.1 OR 3.11

To install INTERFACT:

1 Put the disk in the floppy drive

2 Select RUN from the FILE menu in the PROGRAM MANAGER

3 Type **A:\INSTALL** (Where A is the letter of your floppy drive)

4 Click OK – unless you want to change the name of the INTERFACT directory

To run INTERFACT:

Once the program has installed, open the INTERFACT group in the PROGRAM MANAGER and double click on the icon called RAINFORESTS

PC WITH WINDOWS 95

To install INTERFACT:

1 Put the disk in the floppy drive

2 Select RUN from the START menu

3 Type **A:\INSTALL** (Where A is the letter of your floppy drive)

4 Click OK – unless you want to change the name of the INTERFACT directory

To run INTERFACT:

Once the program has installed, open the START menu and select PROGRAMS then select INTERFACT and click on the icon called RAINFORESTS

APPLE MAC

To install INTERFACT:

1 Put the disk in the floppy drive

2 Double click on the icon called INTERFACT INSTALLER

3 Click CONTINUE

4 Click INSTALL – unless you want to change the name of the INTERFACT folder

To run INTERFACT:

Once the program has installed, open the INTERFACT folder and double click on the icon called RAINFORESTS

How to use INTERFACT

INTERFACT is easy to use.
First find out how to run the program
(see page 40) then read these simple
instructions and dive in!

You will find that there are lots of different features to explore.
To select one, operate the controls on the right hand side of the screen. You will see that the main area of the screen changes as you click on to different features.

For example, this is what your screen will look like when you select Go Bananas, a fun-filled test of your rainforest knowledge. Once you've chosen a feature, click on the main screen to start playing.

Click here to select the feature you want to play.

Click to continue

Click on the arrow keys to scroll through the different features on the disk or find your way to the exit.

This is the reading box where instructions and directions appear explaining what to do. Go to page 4 to find out what's on the disk.

DISK LINKS

When you read the book, you'll come across Disk Links. These show you where to find activities on the disk that relate to the page you are reading. Use the arrow keys to find the icon on screen that matches the one in the Disk Link.

DISK LINK
Build a rainforest food web and find out who eats what!

BOOKMARKS

As you play the features on the disk, you'll bump into Bookmarks. These show you where to look in the book for more information about the topic on screen. Just turn to the page of the book shown in the Bookmark.

23

WORK BOOK

On pages 36-39 you'll find note pages to photocopy and use again and again. Use them to write down your own discoveries as you go through the book and the disk.

HOT DISK TIPS

- After you have chosen the feature you want to play, remember to move the cursor from the icon to the main screen before clicking on the mouse again.

- If you don't know how to use one of the on-screen controls, simply touch it with your cursor. An explanation will pop up in the reading box!

- Keep a close eye on the cursor. When it changes from an arrow ➡ to a hand ☞ click your mouse and something will happen.

- Any words that appear on screen in blue and underlined are "hot". This means you can touch them with the cursor for more information.

- Explore the screen! There are secret hot spots and hidden surprises to find.

Troubleshooting

If you have a problem with the INTERFACT disk, you should find the solution here. You can also call the helpline on 0171 684 4050. The lines are open from 10am to 5pm, Monday to Friday and calls are charged at normal rates. But remember to get permission from the person who pays the bill before you use the phone

QUICK FIXES Run through these general checkpoints before consulting COMMON PROBLEMS (see opposite page).

QUICK FIXES

PC WITH WINDOWS 3.1 OR 3.11

1 Check that you have the minimum specification: 386/33Mhz, VGA colour monitor, 4Mb of RAM.

2 Make sure you have typed in the correct instructions: a colon (:) not a semi-colon (;) and a back slash (\) not a forward slash (/). Also, do not put any spaces between letters or punctuation.

3 It is important that you do not have any other programs running. Before you start **INTERFACT**, hold down the Control key and press Escape. If you find that other programs are open, click on them with the mouse, then click the End Task key.

QUICK FIXES

PC WITH WINDOWS 95

1 Make sure you have typed in the correct instructions: a colon (:) not a semi-colon (;) and a back slash(\) not a forward slash (/).
Also, do not put any spaces between letters or punctuation.

2 It is important that you do not have any other programs running. Before you start **INTERFACT**, look at the task bar. If you find that other programs are open, click on them with the right mouse button and select Close from the pop-up menu.

APPLE MAC

1 Make sure that you have the minimum specification: 68020 processor, 640x480 colour display, system 7.0 (or a later version) and 4Mb of RAM.

2 It is important that you do not have any other programs running. Before you start **INTERFACT**, click on the application menu in the top right-hand corner. Select each of the open applications and select Quit from the File menu.

COMMON PROBLEMS

Symptom: Cannot load disk.
Problem: There is not enough space available on your hard disk.
Solution: Make more space available by deleting old applications and programs you don't use until 6Mb of free space is available.

Symptom: Disk will not run.
Problem: There is not enough memory available.
Solution: *Either* quit other applications and programs (see Quick Fixes) *or* increase your machine's RAM by adjusting the Virtual Memory.

Symptom: Graphics do not load or are poor quality.
Problem: *Either* there is not enough memory available *or* you have the wrong display setting.
Solution: *Either* quit other applications and programs (see Quick Fixes) *or* make sure that your monitor control is set to 256 colours (MAC) or VGA (PC).

Symptom: There is no sound (PCs only).
Problem: Your sound card is not Soundblaster compatible.
Solution: Configure sound settings to make them Soundblaster compatible (see your sound card manual for more information).

Symptom: Your machine freezes.
Problem: There is not enough memory available.
Solution: *Either* quit other applications and programs (see Quick Fixes) *or* increase your machine's RAM by adjusting the Virtual Memory.

Symptom: Text does not fit neatly into boxes and 'hot' copy does not bring up extra information.
Problem: Standard fonts on your computer have been moved or deleted.
Solution: Re-install standard fonts. The PC version requires Arial; the Mac version requires Helvetica. See your computer manual for further information.

Index

E

eagle 16, 33
ebony 20
environments 10
epiphytes 12
equator 10
extinction 27

F

floppy disks 40–41
Flora Flip 5
flowers 11, 12, 14, 15, 19
flying fox 15
flying mammals 15
Food For Thought 4
forest floor 8, 12, 16, 17, 20, 24
frog 12, 13, 16, 20, 33
fruit 11, 14, 15, 18, 20, 21
fruit bat 15

G

giant eagles 16, 33
Go Bananas! 5

H

hardwoods 20, 22
harpy eagle 16
Help Screen 4
hummingbird 15

I

industrial countries 22, 26
insects 8, 14, 15, 16, 17, 21, 33
It's A Jungle Out There 5

J

jaguar 16

K

Kayapo Indians 27

L

lichen 12
lizard 14, 16
Loading instructions for
your disk 40–41

M

mahogany 20
margay 16
medicine 20, 21
mineral reserves 22
minimum specification 40, 44–45
monkey 16
monkey-eating eagle 16
moss 12